Ever After High

A Spelltacular Year

EDDA USA

A Spelltacular Year

Author: Megan Todd
Layout and design: Baddydesign
Printed in India

Distributed by Macmillan

ISBN: 978-1-94078-753-4

www.eddausa.com

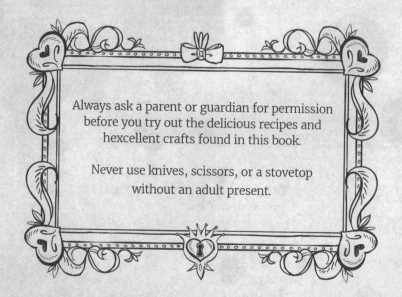

Always ask a parent or guardian for permission before you try out the delicious recipes and hexcellent crafts found in this book.

Never use knives, scissors, or a stovetop without an adult present.

List of Contents

Goal-setting...................................... 4

Yearbook... 8

Crystal Winter's Salted Caramel
   Hot Chocolate............................12

Prince Charming Qualities................14

Storybook Bouquet Activity............. 16

Character Quiz..................................18

Time Flies... 22

Lucky Charm.................................... 24

Princess Pea Butter Sandwich
   Recipe..26

April Fool's Pranks 28

Fairytale Jokes 30

Dragon Egg Bath Bomb Craft.......... 32

Labyrinth Hedge Maze..................... 34

Ashlynn's Diary................................. 36

Fancy Frames Family Tree...............40

Throw Your Own Tea Party 44

Tea Party Invitation 46

Powerful Qualities............................48

DIY Story 50

Wonderlandian Riddles.................... 54

What Do you Believe in? 56

Enchanted Mirrorcraft 58

Raven & Nevermore........................... 60

Who Said What? Quiz.......................62

Oh Curses Moment 66

Hearts Game.................................... 68

Dragon Word Search 72

Happily Ever After 74

Blondie's Guide to School Success ..76

Princessology 101............................. 78

Hextbook Cover Craft....................... 80

Briar's Beauty Rest 82

Apple's Apple Rose Tarts.................. 84

Glitter Pumpkins 88

Your Magic Touch 90

How to Make Your Space Magical ... 92

Raven's Birthday Diary 94

Spelltacular Thank You Notes 98

Best Friends Forever After............. 100

Spelltacular Wishlist 102

Winter in a Bottle 104

Year in Review................................ 106

Notes.. 110

Goal-setting

Your Happily Ever After starts now!

Each new year brings with it the opportunity to write a brand new chapter in the story of your life. One way you can have the best year ever after is by setting goals that can help make your dreams become a reality.

There's no dream that's too big or too small. You're writing your own destiny here — the choice is yours!

Dreams

_____

_____

_____

_____

No matter what dreams you have, figuring out how to make them a reality can be a little tricky. This is where the power of goal-setting can help your life become the stuff of legends. When setting goals, try to make them specific. That way you'll know exactly when you have achieved them. If you're a dancer like Duchess Swan, you may want to be the best dancer ever after. When it comes to your goal-setting, instead of writing, "I want to be a better dancer," try, "I want to give a flawless performance at the spring recital."

Goals

_____

_____

_____

Next, break down your goal even further by writing down the steps you can take to achieve it. This makes it more manageable. For example, "10 minutes of extra practice everyday" or "make sure to stretch every morning" would be good choices for an aspiring dancer.

Steps

_____

_____

_____

_____

Every time that you complete a step, you'll see that you're that much closer to your dream. You'll realize your most magical destiny in no time! So get out there and start doing

—this is Where Your Story Begins!

Year 20____

(date) **Monday**

(date) **Tuesday**

(date) **Wednesday**

(date) **Thursday**

(date) **Friday**

(date) **Saturday**

(date) **Sunday**

6

Year **20**____

date **Monday**

date **Tuesday**

date **Wednesday**

date **Thursday**

date **Friday**

date **Saturday**

date **Sunday**

7

I Rule THE SCHOOL

Ever After High

Yearbook

Wouldn't it be spelltacular to be a student at Ever After High?

Drinking Hocus Lattes with your best friends forever after. Getting totally hexcellent grades in Grimmnastics and Geografairy. Imagine yourself there by creating your very own yearbook entry!

Draw your most fableous portrait here, or paste a particularly enchanting photo.

BIRTHDAY:

FAVORITE SUBJECT IN SCHOOL:

FAVORITE FOOD:

BEST FRIEND FOREVER AFTER:

FAVORITE QUOTE:

Year 20___

(date) Monday

_____
_____

(date) Tuesday

_____
_____

(date) Wednesday

_____
_____

(date) Thursday

_____
_____

(date) Friday

_____
_____

(date) Saturday

_____
_____

(date) Sunday

_____
_____

date **Monday**

_____

_____

date **Tuesday**

_____

_____

date **Wednesday**

_____

_____

date **Thursday**

_____

_____

date **Friday**

_____

_____

date **Saturday**

_____

_____

date **Sunday**

_____

_____

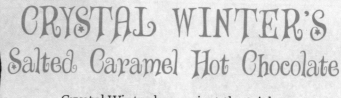

CRYSTAL WINTER'S
Salted Caramel Hot Chocolate

Crystal Winter knows just the trick to beating the winter chill. Cozy up with her special recipe for Salted Caramel Hot Chocolate.
Your taste buds are sure to be enchanted!

(Serves two powerful princesses)

What You'll Need

· 2 mugs
· Small saucepan
· Whisk
· 2 cups milk
· 2 teaspoons sugar
· 7 ounces dark chocolate, broken into squares
· Caramel sauce
· Whipped cream in a can
· Sea salt

Directions

1. Combine all the ingredients in a small saucepan. Heat on the stove at a low setting. As it heats, whisk until well-mixed. Keep stirring frequently. After a few minutes, gently raise the temperature to medium high. Remove from heat and turn off the stove just before the mixture comes to a boil.

2. Drizzle the caramel sauce around the inside of each mug.

3. Carefully pour the hot chocolate and top with whipped cream.

4. Drizzle more caramel sauce over the whipped cream and finish by sprinkling 1–2 pinches of sea salt on top!

Year 20*____

date Monday

date Tuesday

date Wednesday

date Thursday

date Friday

date Saturday

date Sunday

13

Prince Charming Qualities

What makes the perfect Prince Charming?

Some, like Daring Charming, are athletic, brave, and handsome. While others are helpful, outdoorsy, and love animals, like Hunter does.

Pick 5 qualities from the list below that your Prince Charming would have.

Kind	Generous
Mysterious	Imaginative
Confident	Outdoorsy
Courageous	Good cook
Bookworm	Curious
Musical	Honest
Athletic	Talkative
Clever	Optimistic
Funny	Open-minded
Smart	Helpful
Playful	Handsome
Lucky	Stylish
Animal lover	Popular
Caring	Dependable

date Monday

date Tuesday

date Wednesday

date Thursday

date Friday

date Saturday

date Sunday

Storybook Bouquet Activity

What You'll Need

- A page from an old book (you can also print a story of your choosing onto the front and back of a standard sheet of paper)
- Pen or pencil
- Scissors
- Craft glue

Directions

1. Draw a spiral that is approximately 5"x5" onto the book page.
2. Starting at the outside edge of the spiral, cut along the lines that you have drawn.
3. Place a very small drop of glue onto the outside edge of the spiral and start rolling the spiral tightly.
4. After you have rolled up the entire length of paper, place another drop of glue to secure the end of your rose.
5. Hold tightly for a few moments until the glue has partially dried.

(date) **Monday**

_____
_____
_____

(date) **Tuesday**

_____
_____
_____

(date) **Wednesday**

_____
_____
_____

(date) **Thursday**

_____
_____
_____

(date) **Friday**

_____
_____
_____

(date) **Saturday**

_____
_____
_____

(date) **Sunday**

_____
_____
_____

Character Quiz

Are you confidently rebellious like Raven? Do you want to live your life to the fullest like Briar? Or are you at times a little riddle-diculous like Madeline? Take this quiz and find out which Ever After High student you've got the most in common with!

1. It looks like Baba Yaga has been assigned to be your new advisor! Which one of her class and activity suggestions sounds the most hexcellent to you?

A. a Kingdom Magicment. I'm not just another fair face, I've got big destiny planned!

B. Muse-ic. I've got power ballads to sing.

C. Chemythstry. You can never have too many magic potions!

D. Royal Student Council. Thronecoming isn't going to plan itself!

2. What quality do your friends find the most spellbinding about you?

A. I'm fairy sure of myself and know how to get my Happily Ever After.

B. I stand up for myself and my best friends forever after.

C. I have a fableous sense of humor and I get along with everyone!

D. My enthusiasm! I'm here to make the most out of my destiny.

3. You've got a spare moment before you have to be in Grimmnastics class. Where would you like to go for a spell?

A. The Tea Shoppe! Tea is the most tea-rrific thing of the day!

B. The Glass Slipper. Nothing refuels me like a shopping break.

C. My magic mirror. Trying on outfits infront of it is fableous.

D. My dorm room. Sometimes spending time with myself is the most hexcellent way to relax.

4. What activity do you enjoy doing fairy much?

A.   Listening to One Reflection on my MirrorPod.

B.   Drinking tea and speaking in riddles; especially at the same time.

C.   Checking how many likes I've gotten on my latest Mirrorblog post.

D.   Catching up with my friends in the Castleteria.

5. Which color do you find most enchanting?

A.   Royal Red

B.   Amethyst

C.   Aquamarine

D.   Rose

Score

1.   A-0, B-1, C-2, D-3
2.   A-0, B-1, C-2, D-3
3.   A-2, B-3, C-0, D-3
4.   A-1, B-2, C-3, D-0
5.   A-0, B-1, C-2, D-3

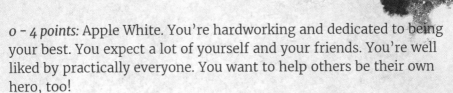

0 - 4 points: Apple White. You're hardworking and dedicated to being your best. You expect a lot of yourself and your friends. You're well liked by practically everyone. You want to help others be their own hero, too!

4 - 8 points: Raven Queen. You're unique and try to always stay true to yourself. Like most independent people, you can sometimes be a little misunderstood, but that's okay because you always win people over in the end! You totally get that everyone is fighting their own battles and that makes you super compassionate about others.

8 - 12 points: Madeline Hatter. In a word, you are tea-rrific! You always see the best in everyone and everything. Your friends and family love your humorous and playful nature.

12 points or more: Briar Beauty. No one holds a candle to your enthusiastic nature. You know that you only live once upon a time, and you're going to live it up every moment! People love that you make the most of every day.

Year 20___

(date) Monday

(date) Tuesday

(date) Wednesday

(date) Thursday

(date) Friday

(date) Saturday

(date) Sunday

Year 20____

(date) **Monday**

(date) **Tuesday**

(date) Wednesday

(date) **Thursday**

(date) Friday

(date) **Saturday**

(date) Sunday

21

TIME FLIES

Ever find yourself bored and impatiently checking your clock, just like Bunny Blanc? Unfortunately, you can't magically make time fly when you find yourself having to wait a spell, but you can play these Ever After High games to speed it up!

The Opposite Game

Make everything you say the opposite of what you mean. See how long it takes for everyone to figure out what you're up to!

Enchanted Mirror

Face a partner and make the wackiest faces you can think of. The other player has to imitate every face you make. The player that gets the other to laugh first wins!

If I Didn't

Like most Wonderlandian games, this one takes a whole lot of cleverness. The first player begins by making a statement. For example, "If I didn't ride a bike ..." The next player has to finish the statement with a rhyme: "... I'd have to take a hike!"

Make up a secret language like Riddlish

Create a code by swapping out words with different ones to make a language that will sound like gibberish to others. For instance, replace door with codfish and girl with banana. "I just saw a banana walk through a codfish!"

(date) **Monday**

_____

_____

_____

(date) **Tuesday**

_____

_____

_____

(date) **Wednesday**

_____

_____

_____

(date) **Thursday**

_____

_____

_____

(date) **Friday**

_____

_____

_____

(date) **Saturday**

_____

_____

_____

(date) **Sunday**

_____

_____

_____

Lucky Charm

How about bottling a bit of your own luck? You'll be totally charmed by this fableous Good Luck Charm craft.

What You'll Need

- A small glass bottle with lid or cap
- Glitter or sand
- Flower petals (one in blue, purple, yellow, orange, red. If you can't find flower petals you can also make them out of tissue paper.)
- A toothpick or tweezers
- Paper
- String

The Steps

1. Fill the bottle halfway with glitter or sand.
2. With a toothpick or tweezers, place the flower petals into the bottle.
3. On a small piece of paper, write down the words "Just like my story, I make my own luck."
4. Roll the paper into a tiny scroll and stick it into the bottle.
5. Tightly seal the lid and keep your bottle handy for whenever you need a little good luck!

date **Monday**

date **Tuesday**

date **Wednesday**

date **Thursday**

date **Friday**

date **Saturday**

date **Sunday**

Princess Pea Butter Sandwich Recipe

One bite of these *Princess Pea Butter Sandwiches* and you'll know why they're a Castleteria fave! Conjuring up your own batch of these delectably charming sandwiches is *easy peasy*.

What You'll Need

- Thin white sandwich bread
- 1 cup frozen peas
- 2 tablespoons of unsalted butter
- 1 tablespoon of cream cheese
- 2-3 sprigs of fresh mint leaves
- Salt, to taste
- Small pot
- Food processor

Directions

1. Boil peas for 2-3 minutes in water until tender.
2. Drain the peas.
3. Add the peas, butter, cream cheese, and mint into the food processor.
4. Whip until the mixture is nice and creamy. Salt to taste.
5. Spread the puree onto bread slices, make a sandwich, cut off the crusts, and enjoy!

date **Monday**

date **Tuesday**

date **Wednesday**

date **Thursday**

date **Friday**

date **Saturday**

date **Sunday**

April Fool's Pranks

This April Fools' Day, take a page from Kitty Cheshire and play some of these mischievous practical jokes on your friends and family!

Watchful Eyes

Stick googly eyes of different sizes to the food in your fridge. Imagine the look on your family members' faces when they open the door to see the jam, eggs, and ketchup looking back at them!

Bug in Ice Cube

Freeze plastic insects, like flies or beetles, with water in an ice cube tray. Sneak one into somebody's drink when they're not looking.

Stuck Coin

Glue a quarter to the sidewalk and hide somewhere nearby to watch as people try to pick it up!

Coffee Paint Cup

On a sheet of wax paper, mix equal parts of white glue and brown paint in a disposable coffee cup. Slowly tip the cup to its side and let the mixture ooze out onto the wax paper. Let dry for a few hours and then peel the cup and paint off of the paper. You now have what looks like an overturned coffee cup mess. Place it on someone's bed or computer for the most hexcellent prank!

Year 20___

date Monday
_____
_____

date Tuesday
_____
_____

date Wednesday
_____
_____

date Thursday
_____
_____

date Friday
_____
_____

date Saturday
_____
_____

date Sunday
_____
_____

29

Fairytale Jokes

After a long week of Damsel in Distressing classes, the students at Ever After High love getting together for tea, scones, and a few laughs at The Mad Hatter's Tea Shoppe. Here are some of their favorite jokes.

How does Hunter Huntsman tie his shoelaces?
With a long bow.

Why didn't Blondie Lockes sleep well last night?
Night-bears!

Why is Snow White such a wonderful judge?
Because she's the fairest of them all.

Why was Cinderella not good at playing Dragon Games?
She always ran away from the ball.

Where did Humphrey Dumpty get a job?
At the eggplant.

Why do dragons sleep all day?
So they can fight knights.

How did Jack know how many beans his cow was worth?
He used a cowculator.

date **Monday**

date **Tuesday**

date **Wednesday**

date **Thursday**

date **Friday**

date **Saturday**

date **Sunday**

Dragon Egg Bath Bomb Craft

When it's time to get your fairest, these fableously fizzy Dragon Egg Bath Bombs will transform bathtime into one spelltacular soak.

What You'll Need

- Plastic Easter eggs
- Latex gloves
- 1 cup baking soda
- ½ cup citric acid
- ½ cup Epsom salt
- Blue food coloring
- Red food coloring
- 2 teaspoons lavender essential oil
- 2 tablespoons olive oil
- One large bowl and three small bowls
- Whisk

The Steps

1. In a bowl, whisk the baking soda, citric acid, and Epsom salt. Add the olive oil, one tablespoon at a time, mixing well. Now, add the lavender oil, mixing well after each teaspoon. Don't let the mixture become too moist in one spot or it will fizz before you want it to.

2. Divide the mixture into 3 separate mixing bowls. In one bowl, add 1 drop of blue. In the next, a drop of red (to get pink). In the third, add one drop each of red and blue to make purple. Mix well to evenly incorporate the colors.

3. Gently pack a bit of the purple mixture into one side of the egg mold, then the blue, and finally the pink. This will create a multicolored effect to your egg. Make sure that you pack each side of the egg molds generously (let them overflow slightly so the mixture can stick to itself). Press together for 15 seconds and then gently unmold. Let the eggs dry for at least an hour.

4. Plop one dragon egg into your bath and watch it fizz like magic!

date Monday

_____
_____
_____

date Tuesday

_____
_____
_____

date Wednesday

_____
_____
_____

date Thursday

_____
_____
_____

date Friday

_____
_____
_____

date Saturday

_____
_____
_____

date Sunday

_____
_____
_____

Labyrinth Hedge Maze

Uh-oh, Earl Grey has wandered a bit too far from the tea shop.
Can you help him get back to Maddie's hat safe and sound?

date Monday
_____
_____
_____

date Tuesday
_____
_____
_____

date Wednesday
_____
_____
_____

date Thursday
_____
_____
_____

date Friday
_____
_____
_____

date Saturday
_____
_____
_____

date Sunday
_____
_____
_____

Ashlynn's Diary

Dear Diary,

What a most page-turning week it has been! Her Majesty the White Queen assigned our most difficult hexam yet and we spent what felt like all of forever after studying for it.

Briar, the best BFFA a girl could ask for, suggested that we hold a study party in the lounge to make things a little more fableous! She always knows how to make the most out of her story! The study party worked like a charm. Not only did we learn every Princessology fact we needed to know, but we had a great time as well! Maddie even brought princess pea butter sandwiches and a big pot of steaming tea!

When we got back to our dorm, I realized that I had made the most terrible mistake. I had been so distracted by the hexam that I forgot to close Sandella's gilded cage! I was beside myself with worry. I haven't been away from Sandella for a single night since spellementary school!

We alerted everyone. Hunter volunteered to check the enchanted forest. Apple and Briar tried the Castleteria, thinking perhaps she had gotten a little hungry. I stayed back and paced the halls in case she found her way back to the room.

That's when I heard Raven shouting for me.

"Ashlynn, you've GOT to see this for yourself!" she called out hexcitedly. She grabbed my arm and led me to the dragon stables.

And what did I see but the most enchanting sight. Sandella sleeping soundly with Nevermore's wing wrapped gently around her. A beautiful new friendship was born!

— Ashlynn

Year 20____

date Monday

_____

_____

date **Tuesday**

_____

_____

date Wednesday

_____

_____

date **Thursday**

_____

_____

date Friday

_____

_____

date **Saturday**

_____

_____

date Sunday

_____

_____

(date) Monday _____

_____

_____

(date) **Tuesday** _____

_____

_____

(date) Wednesday _____

_____

_____

(date) **Thursday** _____

_____

_____

(date) Friday _____

_____

_____

(date) **Saturday** _____

_____

_____

(date) Sunday _____

_____

_____

Fancy Frames Family Tree

Even though they don't have to define your destiny, your family forms a legacy that's an important part of knowing who you truly are, where you come from, and where you want your dreams to take you.

Draw the portraits that make up your fableous family tree.

Below you can find one type of a family tree. You can also draw up your very own tree with the correct number of frames to fit your family!

Year 20___

date Monday

date Tuesday

date Wednesday

date Thursday

date Friday

date Saturday

date Sunday

date **Monday**

date **Tuesday**

date **Wednesday**

date **Thursday**

date **Friday**

date **Saturday**

date **Sunday**

Throw Your Own Tea Party

Welcome spring by throwing a tea party for you and your friends! Here are a few ideas that will make your party tea-riffic!

The very best part of hosting your own tea party is that you can make it uniquely YOU by choosing your favorite decorations and foods. That is exactly why Wonderlandians love it so! If you have these three things covered, your party will be a tea-tastic success.

Nibbles

Choose any of your favorite foods to serve, just make sure that they're dainty and bite-sized. For instance, savory sandwiches cut into tiny rectangles, scones with butter and jam, and mini-cupcakes are all great ideas!

Décor

The table will be more colorful and wonderlandifully whimsical if things are mismatched. Use different plates, napkins, and utensils for a one-of-a-kind look. You can even ask your friends to bring their own teacup!

The tea

There are so many fableous teas that you can serve! Hibiscus is a fruity pink tea that's tart and refreshing — and always a crowd-pleaser. Chamomile is an herbal tea that instantly makes you feel so warm and cozy. And of course, Earl Grey — a true classic! It's a citrusy black tea that's delicious with cream and sugar. No wonder it's Maddie's favorite.

But the most important part of a tea party with your friends is the Wonderlandiful fun and conversation. Don't forget to brush up on your riddles and word games!

Year 20____

date Monday

date Tuesday

date Wednesday

date Thursday

date Friday

date Saturday

date Sunday

45

Tea Party Invitation

These tea inspired invitations will be sure to get all of your guests in the mood for one fableous tea party.

What You'll Need:

- Index cards
- Scissors
- Hole punch
- Colorful string
- Fine tip magic markers
- Ruler (to make straight lines)

Instructions

1. Begin by cutting off two points of each index card to mimic the look of a tea bag. This will be the top of your invitation.

2. Punch a hole at the center of the top.

3. Next, write down the details of your party on the invitations. Be creative.

4. Hexpress your one of a kind style by adding decorative touches to your invitations like drawing swirls, flowers, and hearts. Be sure to include the time and location.

Here's an example:

You are hereby summoned to afternoon tea,
And a most delightful party it's sure to be!
Place: Enchanted Forest
Time: Saturday afternoon, 3:00 pm

You are hereby summoned to afternoon tea,

And a most delightful party it's sure to be!

Place: _____

Time: _____

5. Finish by attaching a piece of string through the punched hole at the top.

Powerful Qualities

The princesses at Ever After High aren't the only ones that can be powerful! Circle the *spelltacular* qualities that make you powerful.

Inspiring	Collaborative	Graceful
Hardworking	Decisive	Ambitious
Dedicated	Motivating	Resourceful
Courageous	Genuine	Nature-loving
Independent	Brave	Helpful
Inventive	Heroic	Athletic
Driven	Strong	Loyal
Generous	Spirited	Protective
Clever	Assertive	Artistic
Curious	Lucky	Honest
Unpredictable	Dependable	Friendly
Funny	Considerate	Smart
Encouraging	Determined	Cheerful
Imaginative	Candid	Enthusiastic
Fun-loving	Enthusiastic	Stylish
Adventurous	Free-spirited	Original
Spontaneous	Helpful	Progressive
Creative	Loving	Bold
Confident	Selfless	

Year 20___

(date) Monday

(date) Tuesday

(date) Wednesday

(date) Thursday

(date) Friday

(date) Saturday

(date) Sunday

DIY STORY

You control the storybook! Choose two characters, a plot, and a place
from each category to make your very own fableous story.

Let your imagination soar!

Characters

Apple White
Raven Queen
Darling Charming
Madeline Hatter
Cerise Hood
Poppy O'Hair
Lizzie Hearts
Cedar Wood
Blondie Lockes

Plot

Find a mysterious object
Lose something valuable
Discover a new portal
Plan a party
Make a new friend
Solve a problem

Place

Mad Hatter's Tea Shoppe
Well of Wonder
The Tower Hair Salon
Multihex Movie Theater
Enchanted Forest
Castleteria

_____ and _____
          (character)   (character)
_____ in/at _____
          (plot)   (place)

_____
_____
_____
_____
_____
_____
_____
_____
_____
_____
_____
_____
_____
_____
_____
_____
_____
_____
_____
_____
_____
_____
_____
_____
_____

Year 20____

(date) **Monday**

(date) **Tuesday**

(date) **Wednesday**

(date) **Thursday**

(date) **Friday**

(date) **Saturday**

(date) **Sunday**

date **Monday**

date **Tuesday**

date **Wednesday**

date **Thursday**

date **Friday**

date **Saturday**

date **Sunday**

Wonderlandian
RIDDLES

Wonderlandians know how to have a riddle-diculously good time! See if you can stump your Best Friends Forever After with these riddles.

What is the longest word in the English language?

Answer: SMILES. There's a "mile" between the first and last letters!

I'm tall when I'm young and I'm short when I'm old. What am I?

Answer: A candle.

What has hands but cannot clap?

Answer: A clock.

What odd number becomes even when it loses its head?

Answer: Seven.

What starts with the letter "t," is filled with "t," and ends in "t"?

Answer: A teapot.

I am the beginning of the end, the end of every place. I am the beginning of eternity, the end of time and space. What am I?

Answer: The letter "e."

(date) **Monday**

_____
_____

(date) **Tuesday**

_____
_____

(date) **Wednesday**

_____
_____

(date) **Thursday**

_____
_____

(date) **Friday**

_____
_____

(date) **Saturday**

_____
_____

(date) **Sunday**

_____
_____

What Do you Believe In?

Hey guys, Raven here. Sometimes it seems like people think that being strong and standing up for what you believe in comes easy. But the truth is, it takes a whole lot of courage to believe in yourself and to choose your own destiny.

Whenever I start to doubt myself, I find it helpful to write down what I believe in. The more I know about me the more I start to truly believe in myself. So don't worry about what other people say. Let them write their own stories while you write yours.

Take a deep breath and remember that you can do anything. We are all capable of greatness!

What are some of the things that you believe in and aren't afraid to stand up for?

_____

_____

_____

_____

_____

_____

(date) **Monday**

_____
_____
_____

(date) **Tuesday**

_____
_____
_____

(date) **Wednesday**

_____
_____
_____

(date) **Thursday**

_____
_____
_____

(date) **Friday**

_____
_____
_____

(date) **Saturday**

_____
_____
_____

(date) **Sunday**

_____
_____
_____

Enchanted Mirror Craft

This spellbinding mirror craft is sure to enchant every time you pick it up! After all, every powerful princess deserves a mirror that is just as fair as she is.

What You'll Need

- A plastic mirror with handle
- Fine-grain sandpaper
- Craft glue
- Hot glue gun with glue
- Paintbrush
- Masking tape
- Newspaper
- Paper bowl or plate
- Glitter (gold or silver)
- Assorted decorative jewels

Directions

1. Gently scratch the plastic parts of the mirror with the sandpaper, using a circular motion. This will help the glue better stick to the plastic.

2. Cut a piece of newspaper that's a wee bit smaller than the reflective surface of the mirror. Use masking tape to attach. Be sure to cover the edges, as this will protect it from the glue and glitter.

3. Squeeze some craft glue onto the paper bowl or plate and apply it with the paintbrush to the backside of the mirror.

4. Generously sprinkle the glitter all over the glue, giving the mirror a nice coating. Shake off any excess. Once dry, do the same to the front of the mirror. (If you can still see the plastic portion of the mirror, repeat this step — you want the mirror to be a solid, glittering object.)

5. Lastly, try out a few designs and patterns with the jewels. When you've decided on the perfect combination, stick them on with hot glue.

(date) Monday

(date) **Tuesday**

(date) Wednesday

(date) **Thursday**

(date) Friday

(date) **Saturday**

(date) Sunday

Raven & Nevermore

Color Raven and Nevermore in enchanting colors.

"Let go of the fear and fly. Rise up:
The sky's the limit now."

(date) Monday

(date) **Tuesday**

(date) Wednesday

(date) **Thursday**

(date) Friday

(date) **Saturday**

(date) Sunday

Who said What? Quiz

So, you think that you're *Ever After High's* most *fableous* fan of all?
See if you can guess which character said these quotes!

"Be cloaked in mystery."

_____

"Like my mom Goldilocks, I like things just right."

_____

"Shuffle the deck of destiny!"

_____

"Sure as a pickle in a hat!"

_____

"I am going to write my own destiny. My own happily ever after. Starting now."

_____

"Being cursed could be worse. Sometimes people make a mistake and tell a lie, at least I never have to worry about that!"

_____

"Every fairytale princess has a special connection to woodland creatures. But I can actually understand what they're saying."

_____

"Everyone is so used to following their destinies, they don't know how to follow their heart. I'm here to change that!"

_____

Answers:

1. Cerise Hood 2. Blondie Lockes 3. Lizzie Hearts 4. Madeline Hatter 5. Raven Queen 6. Cedar Wood 7. Ashlynn Ella 8. C.A. Cupid

Year 2()____

(date) Monday
_____
_____

(date) Tuesday
_____
_____

(date) Wednesday
_____
_____

(date) Thursday
_____
_____

(date) Friday
_____
_____

(date) Saturday
_____
_____

(date) Sunday
_____
_____

(date) Monday

(date) **Tuesday**

(date) Wednesday

(date) **Thursday**

(date) Friday

(date) **Saturday**

(date) Sunday

OH CURSES MOMENT

Everyone at Ever After High has their own *Oh Curses!* moment. Raven can't seem to keep her spells from backfiring. Briar falls asleep at the drop of a hat. Cedar has to tell everyone the truth, whether she wants to or not.

What oh curses moments of yours make you want to shout "Oh my fairy godmother!"?

_____

_____

_____

_____

_____

_____

_____

_____

date **Monday**

date **Tuesday**

date **Wednesday**

date **Thursday**

date **Friday**

date **Saturday**

date **Sunday**

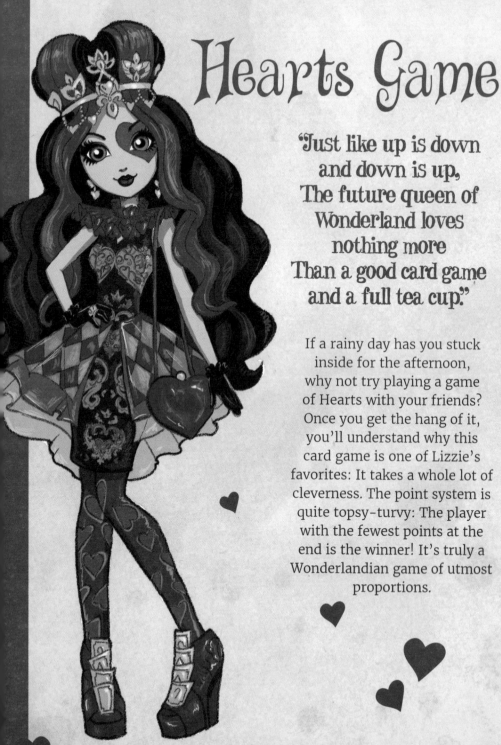

Hearts Game

"Just like up is down
and down is up,
The future queen of
Wonderland loves
nothing more
Than a good card game
and a full tea cup."

If a rainy day has you stuck inside for the afternoon, why not try playing a game of Hearts with your friends? Once you get the hang of it, you'll understand why this card game is one of Lizzie's favorites: It takes a whole lot of cleverness. The point system is quite topsy-turvy: The player with the fewest points at the end is the winner! It's truly a Wonderlandian game of utmost proportions.

How To Play

- Four players make for the perfect game of Hearts. Each player is dealt 13 cards, face down.

- The player that was dealt the two of clubs makes the first move by placing it at the center of the table.

- Next, the player on the left takes their turn, but must follow the suit that the lead player put down; for hexample, a seven of clubs. If a player doesn't have a card in the suit being played, they may play any card they so choose.

- After everyone has played the hand, whoever played the highest card in the suit that was started wins the round, also known as a trick. The winner of the trick (but actually the loser because, remember, Wonderlandians are a bit nonsensical) takes the cards and places them face down. The winner begins the next play, choosing whichever suit suits them the most!

Keeping Score

At the end of each hand, players count the number of hearts they have in their piles. Each heart is worth 1 point, and the Queen of Spades is worth 13 points. Continue until a player reaches 50 points, the highest score making them the loser. Never forget to shout "Off with her head!" at the winner of the game, as a common Lizzie Hearts courtesy, of course.

Year 20____

(date) Monday

_____
_____
_____

(date) Tuesday

_____
_____
_____

(date) Wednesday

_____
_____
_____

(date) Thursday

_____
_____
_____

(date) Friday

_____
_____
_____

(date) Saturday

_____
_____
_____

(date) Sunday

_____
_____
_____

(date) **Monday**

_____
_____
_____

(date) **Tuesday**

_____
_____
_____

(date) **Wednesday**

_____
_____
_____

(date) **Thursday**

_____
_____
_____

(date) **Friday**

_____
_____
_____

(date) **Saturday**

_____
_____
_____

(date) **Sunday**

_____
_____
_____

Dragon Word Search

P	A	C	Y	E	L	Z	A	R	L	I	B	U	D	J
D	Y	Y	X	E	D	D	F	I	U	J	S	A	G	H
B	E	F	G	E	R	O	M	R	E	V	E	N	Y	V
C	Y	E	M	N	M	Z	V	V	Z	C	L	X	G	C
T	N	Y	J	X	I	N	R	Y	B	E	A	R	B	C
D	A	W	Q	A	M	W	R	V	L	Z	C	F	I	Q
U	V	B	V	C	Y	P	O	L	C	M	S	W	L	A
P	N	G	R	E	C	Y	A	R	P	K	F	K	N	D
F	I	G	M	U	E	E	U	Y	E	C	O	E	O	W
D	E	I	J	E	S	M	V	X	S	H	E	A	Q	X
W	Q	M	K	H	P	H	Y	T	E	W	C	P	E	U
X	W	K	L	E	N	S	F	W	I	G	N	N	P	E
R	Z	B	T	J	F	R	Z	I	Y	L	I	N	S	F
K	G	S	Q	S	F	S	A	T	R	L	R	Z	I	D
M	E	X	T	F	C	F	J	S	J	E	P	D	W	T

Can you find all of the Ever After Dragons in this word search?
Check across, down, diagonally, and backwards!

BRAEBYRN   DEEJAY
LEGEND   CRUMPETS
NEVERMORE   BRUSHFIRE
HERO WING   PRINCE OF SCALES

date **Monday**

date **Tuesday**

date **Wednesday**

date **Thursday**

date **Friday**

date **Saturday**

date **Sunday**

Happily Ever After

"We all have the power to choose our stories. And if your choice is to follow your predetermined destiny, you have to trust that it will happen in its own time."
–Raven

Being ready to pledge your destiny is a pretty daunting task. Even though we may not know exactly what our destinies have in store for us just yet, we should never stop dreaming! What do you hope *your* happily ever after will look like?

_____

_____

_____

_____

_____

_____

date Monday

date Tuesday

date Wednesday

date Thursday

date Friday

date Saturday

date Sunday

Blondie's Guide to School Success

Hey guys, Blondie Lockes here. Another school year has begun at Ever After High, and that can only mean one thing: It's time to get your hocus focus on! Whether it's Hexonomics or Geografairy, trying your best will put you on the fast track to achieving your very own Happily Ever After!

Timing is everything

Take a cue from Bunny Blanc! Be sure to get started on your projects way before they're due. That way you'll always feel one step ahead of the work.

Get organized

Lost thronework? Don't know when that Chemythstry project is due? Being disorganized can put a real hex on your grades. Keep your workspace clean. Get a legendary planner (good news: you already have this one, so you're halfway there!) and use it every day.

Ask for help

Let's face it, some subjects come easier than others. When you're struggling, it can really make thronework a drag. Don't be afraid to ask someone that has a better hang of it than you for help.

Stay motivated

This is the most important step of all! Find ways to keep yourself positively enchanted with your studies. Write down a few inspiring quotes to keep them near your workspace. Sometimes you have to remind yourself that it takes a lot of effort to find your Happily Ever After!

date Monday

date Tuesday

date Wednesday

date Thursday

date Friday

date Saturday

date Sunday

Princessology 101

Raven really knows what she's talking about when she says everyone should be able to choose their own Happily Ever After. We should all do what we feel is right and remember to stay true to ourselves, but in a kind and generous way, just like Raven would. Having a truly royal attitude is about being considerate of others and always trying your best.

Here is the first lesson right out of the Princessology 101 hextbook for showing gratitude, thoughtfulness, and compassion.

Gratitude

Never underestimate the power of a thank you. Being thankful will not only make the people in your life feel appreciated, it will also help you remember to always be grateful for all the things that you have.

Thoughtfulness

Let others know that you care by doing little things for them, like sharing a treat or saving them a seat.

Compassion

Give people the benefit of the doubt. Know that everyone is fighting their own battle, and even if they seem more like a villain than a hero, there might be more to their story than you realize.

date Monday

_____
_____
_____

date Tuesday

_____
_____
_____

date Wednesday

_____
_____
_____

date Thursday

_____
_____
_____

date Friday

_____
_____
_____

date Saturday

_____
_____
_____

date Sunday

_____
_____
_____

Hextbook Cover Craft

Cedar Wood loves getting crafty and creative! Get into the back-to-school spirit by transforming your boring textbooks into *hexquisitely* handcrafted *hextbooks* with Cedar's *fableous* tutorial!

What You'll Need

· Decorative paper
· Scissors
· Pencil
· Book

Instructions

Let your imagination fly with the dragons when it comes to designing your cover. You can use Ever After High quotes that inspire you or even make it look like your very own Storybook of Legends!

1. Place paper on a flat working surface, decorative side face down.

2. Open the book you've chosen to cover and place it cover side down onto the paper. Trace the edges of the book with a pen or pencil to use as your template guide

3. Remove the book and cut the paper 1 1/2" above the top and bottom guides, and an extra 3" over the side guides.

4. Fold up the 1-1/2" of paper above the lines you traced along the top and the bottom. Place your book inside the paper. The top and bottom of the book will line up with the edges of the paper.

5. Lay the book down on the paper, and center it. Measure a quarter of an inch from the right-side edge and leave a mark, and do the same on the left side. (That extra space will allow the book to open and close without tearing the cover.) Fold the extra paper on each side to the marks you made and make a crease. Now tuck the front and back of the cover into the pockets.

date Monday

date Tuesday

date Wednesday

date Thursday

date Friday

date Saturday

date Sunday

Briar's Beauty Rest

I'm going to be catching Zs for a hundred years so I guess you could say I know a thing or two about what it takes to be a sleeping beauty. Here are my top five tips that will help transport you to the land of dreams in no time.

Go to bed at the same time every night
Getting your body into a rhythm is a great way to help you get to sleep.

De-clutter your bedroom
You wouldn't think a messy room would matter if your eyes were closed, but sleeping and waking in an orderly space fit for royalty really does make a difference!

Be comfortable
I prefer as many pillows as possible, but you may only like one. Try out different combinations to be sure that you can be your most comfortable.

Try a relaxing scent to help you drift into blissful dreams
Lavender, chamomile, and rose are my favorites! They're sure to make you blissfully fall into your dreams.

Keep it calm
Don't watch TV or use any electronic devices right before bed. Instead, turn down the lights, and read a book instead. Hey, any excuse for more fairytales, right?

Year 20___

date Monday

date Tuesday

date Wednesday

date Thursday

date Friday

date Saturday

date Sunday

83

Apple's Apple Rose Tarts

We all know that Apple White finds *any* food with apples in it irresistible. But these *fableous* tarts are absolute *page-turners* because they look like charming roses when they're done!

(Makes 8 tarts)

What You'll Need

- Muffin pan
- Mixing bowl
- 2 large apples
- 2 sheets frozen puff pastry, thawed
- 1 cup whipped cream cheese
- 3 tablespoons fine sugar
- 2 teaspoons ground cinnamon
- A few pinches of flour

The Steps

1. Preheat oven to 375°F.
2. Cut apple in half, lengthwise, and scoop out the core and remove the stem. With the apple lying flat on the cutting board, slice the apple crosswise thinly, making half moon shapes. Microwave for 3 minutes. This will soften the apple slices so that they'll be easier to roll.
3. In the mixing bowl, combine the cream cheese, sugar, and cinnamon.
4. On a well-floured surface, roll the puff pastry into a larger rectangle and cut vertically into four identical pieces.
5. Spread a thin layer of the cream cheese mixture onto each piece of puff pastry.
6. Stack the apple slices onto the left side of each piece of pastry. Make sure that the peel sticks out over the edge of the pastry. You'll use roughly seven apple slices on each piece.
7. Fold the remaining pastry lengthwise over the apples. Make sure that the apple slices are still peeking out from the pastry.
8. Starting at the bottom, roll the tarts and place into the muffin pan, dough-side at the bottom.
9. Bake for 40 minutes.

Year 20____

(date) Monday

(date) Tuesday

(date) Wednesday

(date) Thursday

(date) Friday

(date) Saturday

(date) Sunday

(date) **Monday**

(date) **Tuesday**

(date) **Wednesday**

(date) **Thursday**

(date) **Friday**

(date) **Saturday**

(date) **Sunday**

Glitter Pumpkins

These glitter pumpkins will add a spelltacular sparkle to your fall holiday décor!

What You'll Need

- Small pumpkins
- White glue
- Paintbrush
- Glitter (you can choose any color you like, or you could mix several together)
- Paper plate
- Masking tape

The Steps

1. Cover the stem of the pumpkin with the masking tape.
2. Apply a thin layer of glue to the top half of the pumpkin.
3. Sprinkle glitter onto the glue. Use the paper plate to catch excess glitter.
4. After the top half of the pumpkin is dry, flip it upside down and repeat for the bottom half.

date **Monday**

date **Tuesday**

date **Wednesday**

date **Thursday**

date **Friday**

date **Saturday**

date **Sunday**

YOUR MAGIC TOUCH

"You are all destined for greatness. There is no such thing as short stories or tall tales."
– Headmaster Grimm

Everyone at Ever After High has their own individual and unique *Magic Touch.* Darling Charming can make time slow down just by tossing her hair. Ashlynn can talk to animals. And Maddie can pull anything out of her hat (literally!).

We all have a *Magic Touch* that's special to us. What's yours?

_____

_____

_____

_____

_____

_____

_____

_____

_____

_____

Year 20___

(date) **Monday**

(date) **Tuesday**

(date) **Wednesday**

(date) **Thursday**

(date) **Friday**

(date) **Saturday**

(date) **Sunday**

91

How to Make Your Space Magical

Is your bedroom décor running a little short on fairy dust and dragon fire? Luckily, shopping at *Throne Furnishings* isn't the only way to add a little magic to your space. It's easy to add spellbinding accents to your bedroom by choosing items with a fantastical touch.

Enchant

No fairytale is complete without an enchanted forest. Bring natural elements indoors and mix them with fanciful touches. Think branches adorned with ribbon, or pretty stones placed in a charming bowl.

Sparkle

There can never be too much twinkle and shimmer in a magical space! Fairy lights, glass bottles filled with glitter, and crystals will instantly turn your room from boring to spelltacular!

Charm

Display your treasures in a charming way by grouping items of similar color or size together. Unexpected items can add a whimsical feel to your space. Try stacking old-fashioned hardback books, or organizing smaller items like jewelry in teacups!

(date) **Monday**

(date) **Tuesday**

(date) **Wednesday**

(date) **Thursday**

(date) **Friday**

(date) **Saturday**

(date) **Sunday**

Raven's Birthday Diary

Dear Diary,

Ever have one of those days that you just know you will never forget? I have to say that I couldn't have been any more hexcited when I woke up this morning. That's because today was my first ever birthday spelleration at Ever After High!

I knew I was going to miss spellebrating such a special day at my home castle with my dad. And that I'd definitely miss all of my favorite foods that Cook always prepares for me, especially sticky salted caramel pudding. But when I overheard Maddie and Cerise planning a "surprise" in hushed tones I just knew it was going to be my best birthday ever after!

Even though I knew my BFFAs had something special planned, there was no way that I could have guessed they would throw such a truly spelltacular party for me!

Ashlynn and Briar completely transformed the Great Hall! Hundreds of enchanted black and purple orbs in all shapes and sizes floated all throughout the grand room. Everything (even the floor!) magically shimmered with silver fairy dust. There were even ice sculptures shaped like swans in every corner of the Great Hall.

After dancing to some hexcellent tunes that Melody Piper was spinning, we sat down to a magnificent feast of roasted beanstalks, butterqueen cakes, snowflake soufflés, and golden gooseberry pies!

Lately, I've really been getting a better hang of my magic. So when Hopper Croakington turned into a frog, after Darling Charming asked him to pass the plum stuffing, I thought helping him turn back to a prince would be the right thing to do. But it was a DISASTER! The spell missed Hopper, and all of the ice sculpture swans changed into actual swans. They started flapping their wings trying to fly and running wild all over the dining tables, the party guests, and of course, our fableous feast. There were feathers in the plum stuffing, droppings in the white pumpkin puddings, and bird tracks in the snowflake soufflés! I was so totally mortified.

Hunter was the first to capture one of the flapping swans. Daring tackled the second. Ashlynn did her best to calm down the other two by talking to them, but all she seemed to do was make them honk more. Luckily Apple sang a lullaby, and that put them RIGHT to sleep.

I thought everyone was more than a little annoyed with me for causing so much chaos. I went back to my room to hide under the covers, but then Cedar, Maddie, and Cerise arrived with a bag of salted caramels. They explained that everyone knew that I was just trying to help out Hopper.

"And besides, who knew that watching Ashlynn try to talk sense to a wild swan could be so fun!" Maddie always knows just what to say to make me feel better.

See diary? I told you it was a birthday spellebration that will DEFINITELY be going into MY story.

-Raven

Year 20____

(date) **Monday**

(date) **Tuesday**

(date) **Wednesday**

(date) **Thursday**

(date) **Friday**

(date) **Saturday**

(date) **Sunday**

date **Monday**

date **Tuesday**

date **Wednesday**

date **Thursday**

date **Friday**

date **Saturday**

date **Sunday**

Spelltacular Thank You Notes

It is the season of *hexpressing* thanks to the people in your life. Grab your fave quill and try out some of these wicked awesome tips on writing the perfect thank you note.

Timing is everything!
The longer you wait to do it, the more difficult it becomes to write.

Details, details!
Include one or two details about the gift or occasion that you enjoyed. For hexample, "Thanks for inviting me to your party! It was so much fun, and you gave out the best goodie bags I've ever received!" or, "The nail polish gift set you gave me for my birthday had the most enchanting colors in it."

Compliments!
Make them feel great by saying something like, "I can't wait to see you again," or, "You always pick out the perfect gift!"

The perfect ending!
Decide on a charming way of giving your regards. "Sincerely" is always a good option, but you could also sign off with "thanks again","with love," or "yours truly."

date **Monday**

date **Tuesday**

date **Wednesday**

date **Thursday**

date **Friday**

date **Saturday**

date **Sunday**

Best Friends Forever After

If you're truly best friends 'till the end, don't you think you should know everything about each other? Grab your BFFA (Best Friend Forever After) and take turns guessing the answers to see who knows the most about the other!

BFFA Interview

1. *Where were you born?*
2. *What is the first thing you do when you get home from school?*
3. *If you had to eat one food for the rest of your life, what would it be?*
4. *Who do you admire the most and why?*
5. *Cedar Wood prefers purple, and Maddie Hatter likes teal. What's the signature color that helps define you?*
6. *Which book have you read more than once?*
7. *What was the name of your first pet?*
8. *Who's your favorite Ever After High character?*
9. *What's the most-played song on your MirrorPod?*
10. *What's your favorite flower?*

Year 20____

date **Monday**

date **Tuesday**

date **Wednesday**

date **Thursday**

date **Friday**

date **Saturday**

date **Sunday**

Spelltacular Wishlist

Would you like a MirrorPod for you and each of your friends?
Or perhaps your own baby dragon in your favorite color? If
your imagination knew no bounds, what would be on your most
spelltacular wish list?

_____

_____

_____

_____

_____

_____

_____

(date) Monday

_____
_____

(date) **Tuesday**

_____
_____

(date) Wednesday

_____
_____

(date) **Thursday**

_____
_____

(date) Friday

_____
_____

(date) **Saturday**

_____
_____

(date) Sunday

_____
_____

Winter in a Bottle

Give your friends a little winter magic this holiday by making them this totally *hexcellent* snowstorm in a bottle.

What You'll Need

- A clear glass jar or bottle with a cap, and the label removed
- Water
- Blue food coloring
- 1 tablespoon glycerin
- Silver glitter
- Snowflake confetti

The Steps

1. Fill bottle ¾ with water.
2. Add 1-2 drops of food coloring.
3. Add the glycerin.
4. Add snowflake confetti and glitter. (The amount you use is up to you. Try closing the bottle and shaking it up to see if you need more.)
5. Fill the rest of the bottle up with water, and shut tightly.

Year 20____

date	Monday
date	Tuesday
date	Wednesday
date	Thursday
date	Friday
date	Saturday
date	Sunday

Year in Review

"The End is Just the Beginning"

Wow, what a seriously fableous year you've had! Write down some of the highlights so you won't ever forget how wicked epic it was!

What hexcellent achievements are you most proud of this year?

_____

_____

_____

_____

What's the most important thing you think you learned this year?

_____

_____

_____

_____

What was your favorite holiday spellebration?

_____

_____

_____

_____

What was the most surprising thing that happened this year?

_____

_____

_____

_____

What was the happiest memory you made for your story this year?

_____

_____

_____

What was the most riddle-diculous thing you saw this year?

_____

_____

_____

What's something you tried for the first time this year?

_____

_____

_____

Year 20___

(date) **Monday**

_____

_____

(date) **Tuesday**

_____

_____

(date) **Wednesday**

_____

_____

(date) **Thursday**

_____

_____

(date) **Friday**

_____

_____

(date) **Saturday**

_____

_____

(date) **Sunday**

_____

_____

(date) **Monday**

(date) **Tuesday**

(date) **Wednesday**

(date) **Thursday**

(date) **Friday**

(date) **Saturday**

(date) **Sunday**

Notes

Notes

Notes